3STORY®

3STORY® participant's guide
PREPARING FOR A LIFESTYLE OF EVANGELISM

[DAVE RAHN & YOUTH FOR C

D1280380

ZONDERVAN®   **Youth Specialties**.com   ZONDERVAN.com/
AUTHORTRACKER
follow your favorite authors

Youth Specialties

3STORY® Participant's Guide: preparing for a lifestyle of evangelism
Copyright © 2006 by Youth for Christ/USA and Dr. Dave Rahn

Youth Specialties products, 300 S. Pierce St., El Cajon, CA 92020 are published by Zondervan, 5300 Patterson Ave. SE, Grand Rapids, MI 49530.

Library of Congress Cataloging-in-Publication Data

Rahn, Dave, 1954-
  3Story patricipant's guide : preparing for a lifestyle of evangelism :
student learning guidebook / by Dave Rahn and Youth for Christ/USA.
      p. cm.
  ISBN-10: 0-310-27374-9 (pbk.)
  ISBN-13: 978-0-310-27374-5 (pbk.)
  1. Christian education—Textbooks for youth. 2. Evangelistic
work—Textbooks. I. Youth for Christ/USA. II. Title.

BV3796.R34 2006
268'.433—dc22

                                                                              2006100233

This edition printed on acid-free paper.

All Scripture quotations, unless otherwise indicated, are taken from the *Holy Bible: New International Version®*. NIV®. Copyright © 1973, 1978, 1984 by International Bible Society. Used by permission of Zondervan. All rights reserved.

The Youth for Christ 3Story® Team included General Editor Jenny Morgan and editors Kevin Becht, Nina Edwards, Wendy Piehl, Don Talley, and Sweena Varghese.

Cover Design by SharpSeven Design
Interior Design by Mark Novelli, IMAGO MEDIA

The 3Story® concept and all 3Story® material copyright 2006 by Youth for Christ/USA®.

Printed in the United States of America

07 08 09 10 11 12 • 23 22 21 20 19 18 17 16 15 14 13 12 11 10 9 8 7 6 5 4 3 2

⠶ CONTENTS

ACKNOWLEDGMENTS

Youth for Christ and Dave Rahn would like to extend very special, humungous thanks to Bill Muir, former vice president of Youth for Christ USA Ministries. We believe that God delivered through Bill many of the best 3Story ideas to YFC and to his kingdom. Thank you, Bill, for more than 25 years of service within YFC, for your amazing creativity in serving students, and for your deep and abiding love for Jesus Christ and his Church. We honor you as YFC's "3Story Grandfather."

We'd also like to offer tribute to Jim Hancock and Todd Temple for their matchless, exceptional contributions to 3Story. Jim and Todd were the brilliant, artistic minds behind the development of 3Story training through YFC's DCLA events. Many thanks to you both! You two made the 3Story story come to life right before our eyes, not to mention right smack in the middle of the hearts of thousands of students!

THE MINISTRIES OF YOUTH FOR CHRIST INCLUDE:

CITY LIFE

YFC's City Life helps young people in urban communities through teaching life skills, building relationships with caring adults, providing opportunities for positive peer group experiences, and sharing the good news of a relationship with Jesus Christ.

TEEN PARENTS

YFC's Teen Parents connects trained adults with pregnant girls and teenage parents in programs designed to help them make good choices and establish a solid foundation in Christ, not only in their lives, but also in the lives of their babies.

YOUTH GUIDANCE

YFC's Youth Guidance reaches troubled young people through juvenile justice and social service agency contacts. Youth Guidance connects them with trained adults who help them make good choices and find healing and new life in Christ.

CAMPUS LIFE

YFC's Campus Life combines healthy relationships with creative programs to help middle school and senior high young people make good choices, establish a solid foundation for life, and positively impact their schools for Christ. Campus Life is a place to make friends, talk about everyday life, and discover the beginning of a life-long relationship with Jesus Christ.

STUDENT LED MINISTRY

Student Led Ministry influences the vision, goals, and practices of Christian students on high school and middle school campuses, encouraging students to live out their faith in the context of their campus community by naturally inviting others to follow Christ with them. Student Led Ministry connects YFC with local churches and other like-minded partners, using adult coaches to help students become authentic, life-long followers of Christ.

YFCAMP (www.yfc.org/camp)

YFC's YFCAMP is a national initiative that exists to create an outdoor environment that invites God to transform the lives of young people through shared experiences, outdoor challenges, and times of solitude.

WORLD OUTREACH (www.yfc.org/worldoutreach)

YFC/USA's World Outreach serves YFC International, sending missionaries to serve as an integral part of indigenous YFC ministries in nations spanning the globe from Bolivia to New Zealand.

PROJECT SERVE® (www.yfc.org/projectserve)

For three decades, YFC's Project Serve has sent thousands of young people and adults on mission trips in partnership with over 90 indigenous YFC ministries.

MYM AND MCYM (www.yfc.org/mym)

YFC's Military Youth Ministry equips ministry centers in the USA with resources and training to reach military youth in their communities. And, in partnership with Military Community Youth Ministries, MYM places youth workers on military bases around the world.

National Internships

YFC is committed to developing emerging leaders in youth ministry. Our national intern program allows college students to spend a summer or school year serving in a local YFC ministry center. The experience ranges from working directly with students to planning and running events, fundraising, helping to lead trips, marketing and communications, and facilitating small groups. For more information, go to www.joinyfc.org.

WELCOME TO THE 3STORY LEARNING EXPERIENCE

If we do this right together, you ought to be able to take it with you. Good learning is like that—portable and offering anywhere, anytime access. Like an iPod. So we're calling these sessions "Learning Pods" or "L-Pods."

This is going to be such a great experience! You should create an official record of who you are and what's going on in your world as you begin to learn a 3Story way of life.

Today's date _____

My name is _____

I go to school at _____

I'm in the_____ th grade.

I'd like it if I learned_____

I'm a little nervous about_____

_____

_____

I think my biggest question right now is _____

_____

_____

I believe my closest friends think my faith is _____

_____

_____

I believe people in my family think my faith is_____

_____

_____

The biggest change in my life over the last year is_____

_____

_____

WHO'S WHO IN MY CIRCLE

NAME _____

SCHOOL _____

GRADE _____

CELL # _____

E-MAIL _____

OTHER INFO. _____

NAME _____

SCHOOL _____

GRADE _____

CELL # _____

E-MAIL _____

OTHER INFO. _____

NAME _____

SCHOOL _____

GRADE _____

CELL # _____

E-MAIL _____

OTHER INFO. _____

NAME _____

SCHOOL _____

GRADE _____

CELL # _____

E-MAIL _____

OTHER INFO. _____

NAME _____

SCHOOL _____

GRADE _____

CELL # _____

E-MAIL _____

OTHER INFO. _____

NAME _____

SCHOOL _____

GRADE _____

CELL # _____

E-MAIL _____

OTHER INFO. _____

NAME _____

SCHOOL _____

GRADE _____

CELL # _____

E-MAIL _____

OTHER INFO. _____

NAME _____

SCHOOL _____

GRADE _____

CELL # _____

E-MAIL _____

OTHER INFO. _____

There is one relationship—our relationship with God—that affects every other relationship in life. So what's the best move you can make—all the time, every time?

WHO DO YOU LOVE?

Write the first name of one friend with whom you intend to share your faith.

_____

How long have you known this person?

_____

How well would you say you know each other? (Mark a place on the line below.)

_____

Barely   Somewhat   Really Well

What do you like best about your friend?

What does your friend know about your faith?

What do you suppose has kept this person from becoming a Christian?

● TAKING THE PLUNGE

Explain how this video relates to the idea of sharing Christ with others.

Which of the attitudes about sharing Christ with others (as expressed by the guy in the boat) have you heard before?

- Which of these attitudes hit closest to home for you?

- Which ones bother you the most? Why?

If you were making a video explaining the right way we should approach swimming and those who can't swim—while knowing it's really talking about evangelism—how would your video be different from what we just saw?

● THREE STORIES

● THREE STORIES

● DIRECTION—MYSPACE NOTES

JOHN 15:4-11

John 15:4

"Remain in me, as I also remain in you. No branch can bear fruit by itself; it must remain in the vine. Neither can you bear fruit unless you remain in me."

John 15:5-8

"I am the vine; you are the branches. If you remain in me and I in you, you will bear much fruit; apart from me you can do nothing. If you do not remain in me, you are like a branch that is thrown away and withers; such branches are picked up, thrown into the fire and burned. If you remain in me and my words remain in you, ask whatever you wish, and it will be done for you. This is to my Father's glory, that you bear much fruit, showing yourselves to be my disciples."

John 15:9-11

"As the Father has loved me, so have I loved you. Now remain in my love. If you keep my commands, you will remain in my love, just as I have kept my Father's commands and remain in his love. I have told you this so that my joy may be in you and that your joy may be complete."

DA VINE CONNECTION

Read John 15:4-11 and answer the following questions.

The words *remain in* are repeated 11 times in this short passage of Scripture. Take a little time to circle those words each time they appear in the text and jot down some thoughts about why Jesus uses these two words so much. What does he want to make sure we understand?

What benefits does Jesus describe for all of us who stay connected to him?

How well connected to Jesus are you? (Mark a place on the line.)

Barely   Comes & Goes   Steady & Strong

What can you do to improve your connection to Jesus?

Finish by praying aloud for what you talked about here:

- That you can understand what Jesus wants you to understand
- That you might experience the benefits of staying connected to Jesus
- That you might improve the strength and frequency of your connection to Jesus

TAKIN' IT TO THE STREETS

Take a few minutes before you leave today to answer the following questions:

WHAT? What was the most significant thing you heard or did or thought about in L-Pod 1?

SO WHAT? Does anything you just wrote down require action?

NOW WHAT? What do you plan to do about that this week?

WHAT TEAM? Whom are you going to tell about your plans so they can help you through prayer and encouragement?

GOD'S STORY—ON YOUR OWN

A Sampler from John's Gospel
The Word Became Flesh (John 1:10-18)

He was in the world, and though the world was made through him, the world did not recognize him. He came to that which was his own, but his own did not receive him. Yet to all who did receive him, to those who believed in his name, he gave the right to become children of God—children born not of natural descent, nor of human decision or a husband's will, but born of God.

The Word became flesh and made his dwelling among us. We have seen his glory, the glory of the one and only Son, who came from the Father, full of grace and truth.

(John testified concerning him. He cried out, saying, "This is he of whom I said, 'He who comes after me has surpassed me because he was before me.'") Out of his fullness we have all received grace in place of grace already given. For the law was given through Moses; grace and truth came through Jesus Christ. No one has ever seen God, but the one and only Son, who is himself God and is in closest relationship with the Father, has made him known.

HMMM...
What difference does it make to you that Jesus delivered grace and truth in his person?

GOD'S STORY—ON YOUR OWN

A Sampler from John's Gospel
Swap Meet (John 2:12-22)

After this he went down to Capernaum with his mother and brothers and his disciples. There they stayed for a few days.

When it was almost time for the Jewish Passover, Jesus went up to Jerusalem. In the temple courts he found people selling cattle, sheep and doves, and others sitting at tables exchanging money. So he made a whip out of cords, and drove all from the temple courts, both sheep and cattle; he scattered the coins of the money changers and overturned their tables. To those who sold doves he said, "Get these out of here! Stop turning my Father's house into a market!"

His disciples remembered that it is written: "Zeal for your house will consume me."

The Jews then responded to him, "What sign can you show us to prove your authority to do all this?"

Jesus answered them, "Destroy this temple, and I will raise it again in three days."

They replied, "It has taken forty-six years to build this temple, and you are going to raise it in three days?" But the temple he had spoken of was his body. After he was raised from the dead, his disciples recalled what he had said. Then they believed the Scripture and the words that Jesus had spoken.

HMMM...
What sorts of things do you encounter that would make Jesus angry enough to take action—like he did in this passage?

GOD'S STORY—ON YOUR OWN

A Sampler from John's Gospel
Nick at Night (John 3:1-21)

Now there was a Pharisee, a man named Nicodemus who was a member of the Jewish ruling council. He came to Jesus at night and said, "Rabbi, we know that you are a teacher who has come from God. For no one could perform the signs you are doing if God were not with him."

Jesus replied, "Very truly I tell you, no one can see the kingdom of God without being born again."

"How can anyone be born when they are old?" Nicodemus asked. "Surely they cannot enter a second time into their mother's womb to be born!"

Jesus answered, "Very truly I tell you, no one can enter the kingdom of God without being born of water and the Spirit. Flesh gives birth to flesh, but the Spirit gives birth to spirit. You should not be surprised at my saying, 'You must be born again.' The wind blows wherever it pleases. You hear its sound, but you cannot tell where it comes from or where it is going. So it is with everyone born of the Spirit."

"How can this be?" Nicodemus asked.

"You are Israel's teacher," said Jesus, "and do you not understand these things? Very truly I tell you, we speak of what we know, and we testify to what we have seen, but still you people do not accept our testimony. I have spoken to you of earthly things and you do not believe; how then will you believe if I speak of heavenly things? No one has ever gone into heaven except the one who came from heaven—the Son of Man. Just as Moses lifted up the snake in the wilderness, so the Son of Man must be lifted up, that everyone who believes may have eternal life in him.

"For God so loved the world that he gave his one and only Son, that whoever believes in him shall not perish but have eternal life. For God did not send his Son into the world to condemn the world, but to save the world through him. Whoever believes in him is not condemned, but whoever does not believe stands condemned already because they have not believed in the name of God's one and only Son. This is the verdict: Light has come into the world, but people loved darkness instead of light because their deeds were evil. All those who do evil hate the light, and will not come into the light for fear that their deeds will be exposed. But those who live by the truth come into the light, so that it may be seen plainly that what they have done has been done in the sight of God."

HMMM...
Can you think of another illustration that describes how different life in the kingdom of God is from our natural, physical existence?

Your friends will most likely consider their own relationships with God when they feel safe to do so. So how can you make it safe by showing them the truth about your own relationship with Jesus?

● BE REAL—MYSPACE NOTES

BE REAL RULES

Tips for being real with your friend

- Don't make things sound better or worse or other than they truly are.

- Don't hold back on the exact nature of your weaknesses and wrongdoing. Do edit the gory details out of respect for your friend.

- Tell your story, not what someone else did to you.

- Describe your motives without making excuses.

- Respect your friend's privacy and, if it matters, ask for the same respect.

- Seek first to understand—not judge nor fix—your friend.

PRACTICE: BE REAL—GUIDED CONVERSATION #1

You and your partner will both answer each question, but you'll alternate going first. (That means the second person who answers question one will be first to answer question two.)

- Take about a minute to tell me about the members of your family.

- Take about a minute to describe something you lacked as a child (something good that you didn't have).

- Describe the first time you recall feeling guilty. (It doesn't have to be literally the first time, just the first time you can remember.)

  - Looking back, why do you think you felt guilty?

  - Tell me how that turned out.

- Describe something that keeps tripping you up (an attitude, a behavior, a habit, a weakness, a craving).

    - Why do you think that's been an issue for you?

    - How is that working out for you now?

- Tell me about something you did recently that hurt you or someone else.

    - How is that working out?

● TAKIN' IT TO THE STREETS

Take a few minutes before you leave today to answer the following questions:

WHAT? What was the most significant thing you heard or did or thought about in L-Pod 2?

SO WHAT? Does anything you just wrote down require action?

NOW WHAT? What do you plan to do about that this week?

WHAT TEAM? Whom are you going to tell about your plans so they can help you through prayer and encouragement?

GOD'S STORY—ON YOUR OWN

A Sampler from John's Gospel
Woman@The Well.com (John 4:1-42)

Now Jesus learned that the Pharisees had heard that he was gaining and baptizing more disciples than John—although in fact it was not Jesus who baptized, but his disciples. So he left Judea and went back once more to Galilee.

Now he had to go through Samaria. So he came to a town in Samaria called Sychar, near the plot of ground Jacob had given to his son Joseph. Jacob's well was there, and Jesus, tired as he was from the journey, sat down by the well. It was about noon.

When a Samaritan woman came to draw water, Jesus said to her, "Will you give me a drink?" (His disciples had gone into the town to buy food.)

The Samaritan woman said to him, "You are a Jew and I am a Samaritan woman. How can you ask me for a drink?" (For Jews do not associate with Samaritans.)

Jesus answered her, "If you knew the gift of God and who it is that asks you for a drink, you would have asked him and he would have given you living water."

"Sir," the woman said, "you have nothing to draw with and the well is deep. Where can you get this living water? Are you greater than our father Jacob, who gave us the well and drank from it himself, as did also his sons and his flocks and herds?"

Jesus answered, "Everyone who drinks this water will be thirsty again, but those who drink the water I give them will never thirst. Indeed, the water I give them will become in them a spring of water welling up to eternal life."

The woman said to him, "Sir, give me this water so that I won't get thirsty and have to keep coming here to draw water."

He told her, "Go, call your husband and come back."

"I have no husband," she replied.

Jesus said to her, "You are right when you say you have no husband. The fact is, you have had five husbands, and the man you now have is not your husband. What you have just said is quite true."

"Sir," the woman said, "I can see that you are a prophet. Our ancestors worshiped on this mountain, but you Jews claim that the place where we must worship is in Jerusalem."

"Woman," Jesus replied, "believe me, a time is coming when you will worship the Father neither on this mountain nor in Jerusalem. You Samaritans worship what you do not know; we worship what we do know, for salvation is from the Jews. Yet a time is coming and has now come when the true worshipers will worship the Father in the Spirit and in truth, for they are the kind of worshipers the Father seeks. God is spirit, and his worshipers must worship in the Spirit and in truth."

The woman said, "I know that Messiah" (called Christ) "is coming. When he comes, he will explain everything to us."

Then Jesus declared, "I, the one speaking to you—I am he."

Just then his disciples returned and were surprised to find him talking with a woman. But no one asked, "What do you want?" or "Why are you talking with her?"

Then, leaving her water jar, the woman went back to the town and said to the people, "Come, see a man who told me everything I ever did. Could this be the Messiah?" They came out of the town and made their way toward him.

Meanwhile his disciples urged him, "Rabbi, eat something."

But he said to them, "I have food to eat that you know nothing about."

Then his disciples said to each other, "Could someone have brought him food?"

"My food," said Jesus, "is to do the will of him who sent me and to finish his work. Don't you have a saying, 'It's still four months until harvest'? I tell you, open your eyes and look at the fields! They are ripe for harvest. Even now those who reap draw their wages, even now they harvest the crop for eternal life, so that the sower and the reaper may be glad together. Thus the saying 'One sows and another reaps' is true.

I sent you to reap what you have not worked for. Others have done the hard work, and you have reaped the benefits of their labor."

Many of the Samaritans from that town believed in him because of the woman's testimony, "He told me everything I ever did." So when the Samaritans came to him, they urged him to stay with them, and he stayed two days. And because of his words many more became believers.

They said to the woman, "We no longer believe just because of what you said; now we have heard for ourselves, and we know that this man really is the Savior of the world."

HMMM...

Imagine you're the person having this conversation with Jesus. At which point would you most likely get nervous, and is there a different point when you'd become excited with hope?

GOD'S STORY—ON YOUR OWN

A Sampler from John's Gospel
Everyone Outta the Pool (John 5:1-15)

Some time later, Jesus went up to Jerusalem for one of the Jewish festivals. Now there is in Jerusalem near the Sheep Gate a pool, which in Aramaic is called Bethesda and which is surrounded by five covered colonnades. Here a great number of disabled people used to lie—the blind, the lame, the paralyzed. One who was there had been an invalid for thirty-eight years. When Jesus saw him lying there and learned that he had been in this condition for a long time, he asked him, "Do you want to get well?"

"Sir," the invalid replied, "I have no one to help me into the pool when the water is stirred. While I am trying to get in, someone else goes down ahead of me."

Then Jesus said to him, "Get up! Pick up your mat and walk." At once the man was cured; he picked up his mat and walked.

The day on which this took place was a Sabbath, and so the Jewish leaders said to the man who had been healed, "It is the Sabbath; the law forbids you to carry your mat."

But he replied, "The man who made me well said to me, 'Pick up your mat and walk.'"

So they asked him, "Who is this fellow who told you to pick it up and walk?"

The man who was healed had no idea who it was, for Jesus had slipped away into the crowd that was there.

Later Jesus found him at the temple and said to him, "See, you are well again. Stop sinning or something worse may happen to you." The man went away and told the Jewish leaders that it was Jesus who had made him well.

HMMM...
What insights does Jesus have that lead him to ask a man who's been paralyzed for 38 years, "Do you want to get well?"

GOD'S STORY—ON YOUR OWN

A Sampler from John's Gospel
5 Loaves, 2 Fish, 12 Doggie Bags (John 6:1-15)

Some time after this, Jesus crossed to the far shore of the Sea of Galilee (that is, the Sea of Tiberias), and a great crowd of people followed him because they saw the signs he had performed by healing the sick. Then Jesus went up on a mountainside and sat down with his disciples. The Jewish Passover Festival was near.

When Jesus looked up and saw a great crowd coming toward him, he said to Philip, "Where shall we buy bread for these people to eat?" He asked this only to test him, for he already had in mind what he was going to do.

Philip answered him, "It would take almost a year's wages to buy enough bread for each one to have a bite!"

Another of his disciples, Andrew, Simon Peter's brother, spoke up, "Here is a boy with five small barley loaves and two small fish, but how far will they go among so many?"

Jesus said, "Have the people sit down." There was plenty of grass in that place, and they sat down (about five thousand men were there). Jesus then took the loaves, gave thanks, and distributed to those who were seated as much as they wanted. He did the same with the fish.

When they had all had enough to eat, he said to his disciples, "Gather the pieces that are left over. Let nothing be wasted." So they gathered them and filled twelve baskets with the pieces of the five barley loaves left over by those who had eaten.

After the people saw the sign Jesus performed, they began to say, "Surely this is the Prophet who is to come into the world." Jesus, knowing that they intended to come and make him king by force, withdrew again to a mountain by himself.

HMMM...
Jesus knows he's going to feed this crowd, but he asks Philip the question anyway. What question could Jesus ask to test you about the stuff in your life?

If your friends are to realize their need for Jesus, they need to encounter him for themselves. So how can you help them experience the power of God as you relate to them?

● PRACTICE: DEPEND ON JESUS— GUIDED CONVERSATION #2

You'll both answer each question, but you'll alternate going first (that means the second person who answers question one will be the first to answer question two).

- Talk for a minute about the high points at school last year.

- Give me 60 seconds on your low points at school last year.

- If I asked you to tell me why you need grace from God right now (not two years or two months ago, but today), what would you talk about?

  - Without going into gory details, tell me about the last time you failed to live up to what you know was right and good in your head and in your heart.

  - Has that problem gone away in your mind? If not, why not?

FOUR CORNER PRAYING

PHYSICAL

SOCIAL

"God, please show me
how I already
depend on Jesus
in each area of my life."

"God, please show me
how I need to
depend more on Jesus
in each area of my life."

MENTAL

SPIRITUAL

DEPEND ON JESUS—MYSPACE NOTES

THE MARTIAN TEST

(Take this on your own time)

If an invisible man from Mars followed you around all day, how much do you think he'd say you depend on Jesus? (Mark a spot on the line.)

0%   50%   100%

When you depend on Jesus in an ordinary day, what do you do (or not do)?

When you stop depending on Jesus in an ordinary day, what do you do (or not do)?

What gets in the way of depending on Jesus?

●TAKIN' IT TO THE STREETS

Take a few minutes before you leave today to answer the following questions:

WHAT? What was the most significant thing you heard or did or thought about in L-Pod 3?

SO WHAT? Does anything you just wrote down require action?

NOW WHAT? What do you plan to do about that this week?

WHAT TEAM? Whom are you going to tell about your plans so they can help you through prayer and encouragement?

GOD'S STORY—ON YOUR OWN

A Sampler from John's Gospel
Thirsty? (John 7:37-52)

On the last and greatest day of the Festival, Jesus stood and said in a loud voice, "Let anyone who is thirsty come to me and drink. Whoever believes in me, as Scripture has said, rivers of living water will flow from within them." By this he meant the Spirit, whom those who believed in him were later to receive. Up to that time the Spirit had not been given, since Jesus had not yet been glorified.

On hearing his words, some of the people said, "Surely this man is the Prophet."

Others said, "He is the Messiah."

Still others asked, "How can the Messiah come from Galilee? Does not Scripture say that the Messiah will come from David's descendants and from Bethlehem, the town where David lived?" Thus the people were divided because of Jesus. Some wanted to seize him, but no one laid a hand on him.

Finally the temple guards went back to the chief priests and the Pharisees, who asked them, "Why didn't you bring him in?"

"No one ever spoke the way this man does," the guards replied.

"You mean he has deceived you also?" the Pharisees retorted. "Have any of the rulers or of the Pharisees believed in him? No! But this mob that knows nothing of the law—there is a curse on them."

Nicodemus, who had gone to Jesus earlier and who was one of their own number, asked, "Does our law condemn a man without first hearing him to find out what he has been doing?"

They replied, "Are you from Galilee, too? Look into it, and you will find that a prophet does not come out of Galilee."

HMMM...
How important is it to actually be thirsty for life when you come to Jesus?

GOD'S STORY—ON YOUR OWN

A Sampler from John's Gospel
Caught with Their Pants Down (John 8:1-11)

Jesus went to the Mount of Olives. At dawn he appeared again in the temple courts, where all the people gathered around him, and he sat down to teach them. The teachers of the law and the Pharisees brought in a woman caught in adultery. They made her stand before the group and said to Jesus, "Teacher, this woman was caught in the act of adultery. In the Law Moses commanded us to stone such women. Now what do you say?" They were using this question as a trap, in order to have a basis for accusing him.

But Jesus bent down and started to write on the ground with his finger. When they kept on questioning him, he straightened up and said to them, "Let any one of you who is without sin be the first to throw a stone at her." Again he stooped down and wrote on the ground.

At this, those who heard began to go away one at a time, the older ones first, until only Jesus was left, with the woman still standing there. Jesus straightened up and asked her, "Woman, where are they? Has no one condemned you?"

"No one, sir," she said.

"Then neither do I condemn you," Jesus declared. "Go now and leave your life of sin."

HMMM...
If Jesus had reversed the sequence of what he said in verse 11, requiring the woman to leave her life of sin before he tells her he doesn't condemn her, how would the story have been different?

GOD'S STORY—ON YOUR OWN

A Sampler from John's Gospel
Sight for Sore Eyes (John 9:1-41)

As he went along, he saw a man blind from birth. His disciples asked him, "Rabbi, who sinned, this man or his parents, that he was born blind?"

"Neither this man nor his parents sinned," said Jesus, "but this happened so that the works of God might be displayed in him. As long as it is day, we must do the works of him who sent me. Night is coming, when no one can work. While I am in the world, I am the light of the world."

Having said this, he spit on the ground, made some mud with the saliva, and put it on the man's eyes. "Go," he told him, "wash in the Pool of Siloam" (this word means "Sent"). So the man went and washed, and came home seeing.

His neighbors and those who had formerly seen him begging asked, "Isn't this the same man who used to sit and beg?" Some claimed that he was.

Others said, "No, he only looks like him."

But he himself insisted, "I am the man."

"How then were your eyes opened?" they asked.

He replied, "The man they call Jesus made some mud and put it on my eyes. He told me to go to Siloam and wash. So I went and washed, and then I could see."

"Where is this man?" they asked him.

"I don't know," he said.

They brought to the Pharisees the man who had been blind. Now the day on which Jesus had made the mud and opened the man's eyes was a Sabbath. Therefore the Pharisees also asked him how he had received his sight. "He put mud on my eyes," the man replied, "and I washed, and now I see."

Some of the Pharisees said, "This man is not from God, for he does not keep the Sabbath."

But others asked, "How can a sinner perform such signs?" So they were divided.

Then they turned again to the blind man, "What have you to say about him? It was your eyes he opened."

The man replied, "He is a prophet."

They still did not believe that he had been blind and had received his sight until they sent for the man's parents. "Is this your son?" they asked. "Is this the one you say was born blind? How is it that now he can see?"

"We know he is our son," the parents answered, "and we know he was born blind. But how he can see now, or who opened his eyes, we don't know. Ask him. He is of age; he will speak for himself." His parents said this because they were afraid of the Jewish leaders, who already had decided that anyone who acknowledged that Jesus was the Messiah would be put out of the synagogue. That was why his parents said, "He is of age; ask him."

A second time they summoned the man who had been blind. "Give glory to God and tell the truth," they said. "We know this man is a sinner."

He replied, "Whether he is a sinner or not, I don't know. One thing I do know. I was blind but now I see!"

Then they asked him, "What did he do to you? How did he open your eyes?"

He answered, "I have told you already and you did not listen. Why do you want to hear it again? Do you want to become his disciples too?"

Then they hurled insults at him and said, "You are this fellow's disciple! We are disciples of Moses! We know that God spoke to Moses, but as for this fellow, we don't even know where he comes from."

The man answered, "Now that is remarkable! You don't know where he comes from, yet he opened my eyes. We know that God does not listen to sinners. He listens to the godly person who does his will. Nobody has ever heard of opening the eyes of a man born blind. If this man were not from God, he could do nothing."

To this they replied, "You were steeped in sin at birth; how dare you lecture us!" And they threw him out.

Jesus heard that they had thrown him out, and when he found him, he said, "Do you believe in the Son of Man?"

"Who is he, sir?" the man asked. "Tell me so that I may believe in him."

Jesus said, "You have now seen him; in fact, he is the one speaking with you."

Then the man said, "Lord, I believe," and he worshiped him.

Jesus said, "For judgment I have come into this world, so that the blind will see and those who see will become blind."

Some Pharisees who were with him heard him say this and asked, "What? Are we blind too?"

Jesus said, "If you were blind, you would not be guilty of sin; but now that you claim you can see, your guilt remains.

HMMM...
What do you like best about Jesus in this story?

Your friends' desires for God need to be awakened and encouraged. How can you live in such a way that you inspire this kind of seeking?

● THAT LOVE THING

Mark on the target how much you identify with Gabriele's struggle to love.

Gabriele: "If I don't like somebody, there's usually a reason. I can't just turn that off and love them."

Gabriele: "...if it were that easy I'd be doing it already."

Gabriele: "Are you gonna tell me God is stretching my capacity to love by sending me idiots?"

What's your biggest love challenge?

Mark on the target how accurate Sage seems.

Sage: "...not liking somebody doesn't get me off the hook from loving them."

Sage: "I'm saying I can't give what I ain't got. I'm saying if I don't love somebody else, it's because I forget how I'm loved. I forget the water is free. If I don't love freely, it just proves I don't get it yet. Jesus really, really loves me—so much it hurts; so much it, it, it killed him to see me out here dying of thirst; out here eatin' sand. He just really loves me...I'm such a freak, and he just really loves me."

When is it the hardest for you to remember how much God loves you?

When you forget how much God loves you, how does it affect the way you love others?

●LOVE OTHERS—MYSPACE NOTES

NOW THAT'S A PRAYER!

I pray that out of his glorious riches he may strengthen you with power through his Spirit in your inner being, so that Christ may dwell in your hearts through faith. And I pray that you, being rooted and established in love, may have power, together with all the Lord's people, to grasp how wide and long and high and deep is the love of Christ, and to know this love that surpasses knowledge—that you may be filled to the measure of all the fullness of God.

—Ephesians 3:16-19

LOVE-STORMING

Jot down ideas—either your own or ones you hear from others in your Circle—that help you answer the following questions.

What are some ways to love your friends without using words?

What are some ways to love your friends by using some words, but never specifically talking about God or Jesus?

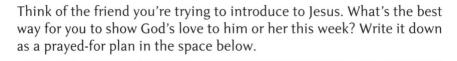

Think of the friend you're trying to introduce to Jesus. What's the best way for you to show God's love to him or her this week? Write it down as a prayed-for plan in the space below.

The best way for me to show God's love to _____
this week is:

● TAKIN' IT TO THE STREETS

Take a few minutes before you leave today to answer the following questions:

WHAT? What was the most significant thing you heard or did or thought about in L-Pod 4?

SO WHAT? Does anything you just wrote down require action?

NOW WHAT? What do you plan to do about that this week?

WHAT TEAM? Whom are you going to tell about your plans so they can help you through prayer and encouragement?

GOD'S STORY—ON YOUR OWN

A Sampler from John's Gospel
Making Metaphors (John 10:1-21)

"Very truly I tell you Pharisees, anyone who does not enter the sheep pen by the gate, but climbs in by some other way, is a thief and a robber. The one who enters by the gate is the shepherd of the sheep. The gatekeeper opens the gate for him, and the sheep listen to his voice. He calls his own sheep by name and leads them out. When he has brought out all his own, he goes on ahead of them, and his sheep follow him because they know his voice. But they will never follow a stranger; in fact, they will run away from him because they do not recognize a stranger's voice." Jesus used this figure of speech, but the Pharisees did not understand what he was telling them.

Therefore Jesus said again, "Very truly I tell you, I am the gate for the sheep. All who have come before me are thieves and robbers, but the sheep have not listened to them. I am the gate; whoever enters through me will be saved. They will come in and go out, and find pasture. The thief comes only to steal and kill and destroy; I have come that they may have life, and have it to the full.

"I am the good shepherd. The good shepherd lays down his life for the sheep. The hired hand is not the shepherd and does not own the sheep. So when he sees the wolf coming, he abandons the sheep and runs away. Then the wolf attacks the flock and scatters it. The man runs away because he is a hired hand and cares nothing for the sheep.

"I am the good shepherd; I know my sheep and my sheep know me—just as the Father knows me and I know the Father—and I lay down my life for the sheep. I have other sheep that are not of this sheep pen. I must bring them also. They too will listen to my voice, and there shall be one flock and one shepherd. The reason my Father loves me is that I lay down my life—only to take it up again. No one takes it from me, but I lay it down of my own accord. I have authority to lay it down and authority to take it up again. This command I received from my Father."

The Jews who heard these words were again divided. Many of them said, "He is demon-possessed and raving mad. Why listen to him?"

But others said, "These are not the sayings of someone possessed by a demon. Can a demon open the eyes of the blind?"

HMMM...

When you think about the sheep's obligations versus the shepherd's responsibilities, how does that make you feel? (Keep in mind that you're a sheep.)

GOD'S STORY—ON YOUR OWN

A Sampler from John's Gospel
Unusual Occurrence at the Cemetery (John 11:1-46)

Now a man named Lazarus was sick. He was from Bethany, the village of Mary and her sister Martha. (This Mary, whose brother Lazarus now lay sick, was the same one who poured perfume on the Lord and wiped his feet with her hair.) So the sisters sent word to Jesus, "Lord, the one you love is sick."

When he heard this, Jesus said, "This sickness will not end in death. No, it is for God's glory so that God's Son may be glorified through it." Now Jesus loved Martha and her sister and Lazarus. So when he heard that Lazarus was sick, he stayed where he was two more days, and then he said to his disciples, "Let us go back to Judea."

"But Rabbi," they said, "a short while ago the Jews there tried to stone you, and yet you are going back?"

Jesus answered, "Are there not twelve hours of daylight? Those who walk in the daytime will not stumble, for they see by this world's light. It is when people walk at night that they stumble, for they have no light."

After he had said this, he went on to tell them, "Our friend Lazarus has fallen asleep; but I am going there to wake him up."

His disciples replied, "Lord, if he sleeps, he will get better." Jesus had been speaking of his death, but his disciples thought he meant natural sleep.

So then he told them plainly, "Lazarus is dead, and for your sake I am glad I was not there, so that you may believe. But let us go to him."

Then Thomas (also known as Didymus) said to the rest of the disciples, "Let us also go, that we may die with him."

On his arrival, Jesus found that Lazarus had already been in the tomb for four days. Now Bethany was less than two miles from Jerusalem, and many Jews had come to Martha and Mary to comfort them in the loss of their brother. When Martha heard that Jesus was coming, she went out to meet him, but Mary stayed at home.

"Lord," Martha said to Jesus, "if you had been here, my brother would not have died. But I know that even now God will give you whatever you ask."

Jesus said to her, "Your brother will rise again."

Martha answered, "I know he will rise again in the resurrection at the last day."

Jesus said to her, "I am the resurrection and the life. Anyone who believes in me will live, even though they die; and whoever lives by believing in me will never die. Do you believe this?"

"Yes, Lord," she told him, "I believe that you are the Messiah, the Son of God, who was to come into the world."

After she had said this, she went back and called her sister Mary aside. "The Teacher is here," she said, "and is asking for you." When Mary heard this, she got up quickly and went to him. Now Jesus had not yet entered the village, but was still at the place where Martha had met him. When the Jews who had been with Mary in the house, comforting her, noticed how quickly she got up and went out, they followed her, supposing she was going to the tomb to mourn there.

When Mary reached the place where Jesus was and saw him, she fell at his feet and said, "Lord, if you had been here, my brother would not have died."

When Jesus saw her weeping, and the Jews who had come along with her also weeping, he was deeply moved in spirit and troubled. "Where have you laid him?" he asked.

"Come and see, Lord," they replied.

Jesus wept.

Then the Jews said, "See how he loved him!"

But some of them said, "Could not he who opened the eyes of the blind man have kept this man from dying?"

Jesus, once more deeply moved, came to the tomb. It was a cave with a stone laid across the entrance. "Take away the stone," he said.

"But, Lord," said Martha, the sister of the dead man, "by this time there is a bad odor, for he has been there four days."

Then Jesus said, "Did I not tell you that if you believe, you will see the glory of God?"

So they took away the stone. Then Jesus looked up and said, "Father, I thank you that you have heard me. I knew that you always hear me, but I said this for the benefit of the people standing here, that they may believe that you sent me."

When he had said this, Jesus called in a loud voice, "Lazarus, come out!" The dead man came out, his hands and feet wrapped with strips of linen, and a cloth around his face.

Jesus said to them, "Take off the grave clothes and let him go."

Therefore many of the Jews who had come to visit Mary, and had seen what Jesus did, put their faith in him. But some of them went to the Pharisees and told them what Jesus had done.

HMMM...
What difference does it make to you that Jesus weeps, even though he knows everything is going to turn out okay?

GOD'S STORY—ON YOUR OWN

A Sampler from John's Gospel
The Father Speaks Up (John 12:20-36)

Now there were some Greeks among those who went up to worship at the Festival. They came to Philip, who was from Bethsaida in Galilee, with a request. "Sir," they said, "we would like to see Jesus." Philip went to tell Andrew; Andrew and Philip in turn told Jesus.

Jesus replied, "The hour has come for the Son of Man to be glorified. Very truly I tell you, unless a kernel of wheat falls to the ground and dies, it remains only a single seed. But if it dies, it produces many seeds. Those who love their life will lose it, while those who hate their life in this world will keep it for eternal life. Whoever serves me must follow me; and where I am, my servant also will be. My Father will honor the one who serves me.

"Now my soul is troubled, and what shall I say? 'Father, save me from this hour'? No, it was for this very reason I came to this hour. Father, glorify your name!"

Then a voice came from heaven, "I have glorified it, and will glorify it again." The crowd that was there and heard it said it had thundered; others said an angel had spoken to him.

Jesus said, "This voice was for your benefit, not mine. Now is the time for judgment on this world; now the prince of this world will be driven out. And I, when I am lifted up from the earth, will draw all people to myself." He said this to show the kind of death he was going to die.

The crowd spoke up, "We have heard from the Law that the Messiah will remain forever, so how can you say, 'The Son of Man must be lifted up'? Who is this 'Son of Man'?"

Then Jesus told them, "You are going to have the light just a little while longer. Walk while you have the light, before darkness overtakes you. Those who walk in the dark do not know where they are going. Put your trust in the light while you have the light, so that you may become children of light." When he had finished speaking, Jesus left and hid himself from them.

HMMM...
What might it look like for you to become like a kernel of wheat today?

Your friends have their own combinations of needs, experiences, hopes, and talents that make them unique. So how can you best discover what makes them tick?

● EXPERT WITNESS

Remember the friend you were thinking about when you wrote out your love plan on page 41 ("Love-Storming"). Answer the following questions with that friend in mind.

On a scale of 1 to 5, with 5 being the most, how well do you think you know your friend? What makes you believe that?

What do you believe is your friend's biggest need? Why do you think that?

What are some connecting points between your story and your friend's story?

From what you've read so far in the gospel of John (or other Scripture, for that matter), what connecting points do you see between your friend's story and God's Story?

What will it take for you to see more connecting points between your friend's story and God's Story?

● THE FIVE LAWS OF LISTENING

1. Somebody has to go first—help your friend feel safe.

2. Don't compete for airtime—listen more than you talk.

3. Some of the best questions have no question marks at the end—make requests without question marks.

4. Say it again—tell your friend what you think you heard so she or he can correct your false perceptions.

5. Gently ask the tough questions—be prepared to answer what you ask.

> To "listen" another person's soul
> into a condition of disclosure and discovery
> may be almost the greatest service that any human
> being ever performs for another.
>
> —DOUGLAS STEERE, GLEANINGS: A RANDOM HARVEST

LISTEN—MYSPACE NOTES

QUESTIONS WITHOUT A "?"

Here's a sample of some ?-less questions. Mark the one(s) that feels most natural to you, or write down a couple of your own.

Tell me about your family.

I'd like to hear more about that.

I'm wondering what that's like.

Tell me how that's working out for you.

Explain to me how that happened.

Describe to me what that felt like.

Tell me what you were thinking.

Talk about why that was important to you.

HOMEWORK TIME!

Practice: Listen—Guided Conversation #3
A Partnership Exercise (to be done on your own time)

Let this be a conversation, not just an interview. Look for a chance to practice it in a natural setting without interruption. There are seven separate requests without question marks below. Use them as a guide, but let the conversation flow naturally. If you make a request and your partner says, "What do you mean?" explain to the best of your understanding. Feel free to go first, if you think that will help.

After your partner speaks, respond from your own experience (but remember Law Two: "Don't compete for airtime").

There's certainly no hurry. We'll practice some more the next time we're together, so enjoy this.

- Tell me what success means in your family.

  - What about failure? Talk about what that means in your family.

- Describe a difficult struggle with failure in your life.

  - Tell me what you've learned through that so far.

- Tell me about your childhood understanding of God.

  - Tell me where you learned that.

  - Describe how that understanding is different today—and how it's the same.

● TAKIN' IT TO THE STREETS

Take a few minutes before you leave today to answer the following questions:

WHAT? What was the most significant thing you heard or did or thought about in L-Pod 5?

SO WHAT? Does anything you just wrote down require action?

NOW WHAT? What do you plan to do about that this week?

WHAT TEAM? Whom are you going to tell about your plans so they can help you through prayer and encouragement?

GOD'S STORY—ON YOUR OWN

A Sampler from John's Gospel
Party of ~~13~~ 12 (John 13:1-35)

It was just before the Passover Festival. Jesus knew that the hour had come for him to leave this world and go to the Father. Having loved his own who were in the world, he loved them to the end.

The evening meal was in progress, and the devil had already prompted Judas, the son of Simon Iscariot, to betray Jesus. Jesus knew that the Father had put all things under his power, and that he had come from God and was returning to God; so he got up from the meal, took off his outer clothing, and wrapped a towel around his waist. After that, he poured water into a basin and began to wash his disciples' feet, drying them with the towel that was wrapped around him.

He came to Simon Peter, who said to him, "Lord, are you going to wash my feet?"

Jesus replied, "You do not realize now what I am doing, but later you will understand."

"No," said Peter, "you shall never wash my feet."

Jesus answered, "Unless I wash you, you have no part with me."

"Then, Lord," Simon Peter replied, "not just my feet but my hands and my head as well!"

Jesus answered, "Those who have had a bath need only to wash their feet; their whole body is clean. And you are clean, though not every one of you." For he knew who was going to betray him, and that was why he said not every one was clean.

When he had finished washing their feet, he put on his clothes and returned to his place. "Do you understand what I have done for you?" he asked them. "You call me 'Teacher' and 'Lord,' and rightly so, for that is what I am. Now that I, your Lord and Teacher, have washed your feet, you also should wash one another's feet. I have set you an example that you should do as I have done for you. Very truly I tell you, servants are not greater than their master, nor are messengers greater than the one who sent them. Now that you know these things, you will be blessed if you do them.

"I am not referring to all of you; I know those I have chosen. But this is to fulfill this passage of Scripture: 'He who shared my bread has lifted up his heel against me.'

"I am telling you now before it happens, so that when it does happen you will believe that I am who I am. Very truly I tell you, whoever accepts anyone I send accepts me; and whoever accepts me accepts the one who sent me."

After he had said this, Jesus was troubled in spirit and testified, "Very truly I tell you, one of you is going to betray me."

His disciples stared at one another, at a loss to know which of them he meant. One of them, the disciple whom Jesus loved, was reclining next to him. Simon Peter motioned to this disciple and said, "Ask him which one he means."

Leaning back against Jesus, he asked him, "Lord, who is it?"

Jesus answered, "It is the one to whom I will give this piece of bread when I have dipped it in the dish." Then, dipping the piece of bread, he gave it to Judas, the son of Simon Iscariot. As soon as Judas took the bread, Satan entered into him.

So Jesus told him, "What you are about to do, do quickly." But no one at the meal understood why Jesus said this to him. Since Judas had charge of the money, some thought Jesus was telling him to buy what was needed for the Festival, or to give something to the poor. As soon as Judas had taken the bread, he went out. And it was night.

When he was gone, Jesus said, "Now is the Son of Man glorified and God is glorified in him. If God is glorified in him, God will glorify the Son in himself, and will glorify him at once.

"My children, I will be with you only a little longer. You will look for me, and just as I told the Jews, so I tell you now: Where I am going, you cannot come.

"A new command I give you: Love one another. As I have loved you, so you must love one another. By this everyone will know that you are my disciples, if you love one another."

HMMM...
If Jesus were to insist on washing your feet today, what would that mean for you?

GOD'S STORY—ON YOUR OWN

A Sampler from John's Gospel
If I Had Just One More Night (John 13:36–14:31)

Simon Peter asked him, "Lord, where are you going?"

Jesus replied, "Where I am going, you cannot follow now, but you will follow later."

Peter asked, "Lord, why can't I follow you now? I will lay down my life for you."

Then Jesus answered, "Will you really lay down your life for me? Very truly I tell you, before the rooster crows, you will disown me three times!

"Do not let your hearts be troubled. Trust in God; trust also in me. My Father's house has plenty of room; if that were not so, would I have told you that I am going there to prepare a place for you? And if I go and prepare a place for you, I will come back and take you to be with me that you also may be where I am. You know the way to the place where I am going."

Thomas said to him, "Lord, we don't know where you are going, so how can we know the way?"

Jesus answered, "I am the way and the truth and the life. No one comes to the Father except through me. If you really know me, you will know my Father as well. From now on, you do know him and have seen him."

Philip said, "Lord, show us the Father and that will be enough for us."

Jesus answered: "Don't you know me, Philip, even after I have been among you such a long time? Anyone who has seen me has seen the Father. How can you say, 'Show us the Father'? Don't you believe that I am in the Father, and that the Father is in me? The words I say to you I do not speak on my own authority. Rather, it is the Father, living in me, who is doing his work. Believe me when I say that I am in the Father and the Father is in me; or at least believe on the evidence of the works themselves. Very truly I tell you, all who have faith in me will do the works I have been doing, and they will do even greater things than these, because I am going to the Father. And I will do whatever you ask in my name, so that the Father may be glorified in the Son. You may ask me for anything in my name, and I will do it.

"If you love me, keep my commands. And I will ask the Father, and he will give you another advocate to help you and be with you forever—the Spirit of truth. The world cannot accept him, because it neither sees him nor knows him. But you know him, for he lives with you and will be in you. I will not leave you as orphans; I will come to you. Before long, the world will not see me anymore, but you will see me. Because I live, you also will live. On that day you will realize that I am in my Father, and you are in me, and I am in you. Whoever has my commands and keeps them is the one who loves me. Anyone who loves me will be loved by my Father, and I too will love them and show myself to them."

Then Judas (not Judas Iscariot) said, "But, Lord, why do you intend to show yourself to us and not to the world?"

Jesus replied, "Anyone who loves me will obey my teaching. My Father will love them, and we will come to them and make our home with them. Anyone who does not love me will not obey my teaching. These words you hear are not my own; they belong to the Father who sent me.

"All this I have spoken while still with you. But the Advocate, the Holy Spirit, whom the Father will send in my name, will teach you all things and will remind you of everything I have said to you. Peace I leave with you; my peace I give you. I do not give to you as the world gives. Do not let your hearts be troubled and do not be afraid.

"You heard me say, 'I am going away and I am coming back to you.' If you loved me, you would be glad that I am going to the Father, for the Father is greater than I. I have told you now before it happens, so that when it does happen you will believe. I will not say much more to you, for the prince of this world is coming. He has no hold over me, but he comes so that the world may learn that I love the Father and do exactly what my Father has commanded me.

"Come now; let us leave."

HMMM...
If it's ever hard for you to accept that the only way to the Father is through Jesus Christ, what do you do with your difficulty?

GOD'S STORY—ON YOUR OWN

A Sampler from John's Gospel
Father, Son, Holy Spirit + You (John 15:18-27)

"If the world hates you, keep in mind that it hated me first. If you belonged to the world, it would love you as its own. As it is, you do not belong to the world, but I have chosen you out of the world. That is why the world hates you. Remember what I told you: 'Servants are not greater than their master.' If they persecuted me, they will persecute you also. If they obeyed my teaching, they will obey yours also. They will treat you this way because of my name, for they do not know the one who sent me. If I had not come and spoken to them, they would not be guilty of sin; but now they have no excuse for their sin. Those who hate me hate my Father as well. If I had not done among them the works no one else did, they would not be guilty of sin. As it is, they have seen, and yet they have hated both me and my Father. But this is to fulfill what is written in their Law: 'They hated me without reason.'

"When the Advocate comes, whom I will send to you from the Father—the Spirit of truth who goes out from the Father—he will testify about me. And you also must testify, for you have been with me from the beginning."

HMMM...
Are you ready to be identified with Jesus as much as this passage describes?

Your friends may eventually come to a place where they'll decide if they're ready to begin a relationship with Jesus. So how can you know—and help them to know—when they're ready to decide?

● PRACTICE: TIES AND TUGS— GUIDED CONVERSATION #4

Part 1

(Note that only you, Partner #1, may look at the Guidebook during this part.)

Let this be a conversation, not just an interview. There are four separate requests without question marks below. Use them as a guide but let the conversation flow naturally. If you make a request and your partner says, "What do you mean?" explain to the best of your understanding. Feel free to go first, if you think that will help.

After your partner speaks, respond from your own experience (but remember Law Two: "Don't compete for airtime").

You have about seven minutes, so there's no need to hurry. We'll keep track of the time for you.

- Assuming that on your best days you take your pain to Jesus for healing, I'd like to know what you do with your pain on your not-so-good days.

    - Tell me how you learned that this other way could bring you at least temporary relief.

- Are you familiar with the idea of do-overs (second chances, making amends)? Tell me how you think do-overs work.

- Tell me what you've learned about being forgiven and about forgiving others.

Part 2

(Note that only you, Partner #2, may look at the Guidebook during this part.)

Let this be a conversation, not just an interview. There are four separate requests without question marks below. Use them as a guide but let the conversation flow naturally. If you make a request and your partner says, "What do you mean?" explain to the best of your understanding. Feel free to go first, if you think that will help.

After your partner speaks, respond from your own experience (but remember Law Two: "Don't compete for airtime").

You have about seven minutes, so there's no need to hurry. We'll keep track of the time for you.

- Talk about how you came to realize your need for a rescuer.

    - Tell me what you tried on your way to trusting Jesus.

    - Tell me about the connecting points you found between God's Story and your story.

- Tell me how you relate with people who don't follow Jesus.

- I'd like to know how you think that's working, in light of what we've been talking about during our 3Story learning.

TIE POINTS

Connecting Stories

Circle two issues you think your friend struggles with. Then look for matches in the list of stories from John's gospel and circle them. (If you can't think of any, jot down any other ideas you have for scenes from God's Story that might connect with your friend.)

Issues (Their Stories)

addiction	envy	meeting expectations	responsibility
anger	evil spirits	pain	revenge
approval	exaggerating	parents	romance
attractiveness	failure	people of different beliefs	seductiveness
being good	false images of God	people of different classes	self-absorption
being judged	family	people of different cultures	self-image
being loved	fantasies	people of different races	self-importance
being right	going to church	people of different religions	self-indulgence
being taken care of	gossiping	people of the opposite sex	self-righteousness
being tricked	greed	people who are addicted	sex
belonging	guilt	people who are rich/poor	standing out
comparisons	illness	performance	status
conformity	intimacy	popularity	success
control	jealousy	power	worthiness
death	knowledge	rejection	
disapproval	lying	relationships	

Episodes (God's Story)

The Big Open (John 1:1-5)	Unusual Occurrence at the Cemetery (John 11:1-46)
John the Baptizer (John 1:6-9)	Better Him Than Us (John 11:47-57)
The Word Became Flesh (John 1:10-18)	Undignified (John 12:1-11)
The Weird Guy (John 1:19-34)	Big Voice (John 12:12-19)
Pete & Andy Meet Jesus (John 1:35-51)	The Father Speaks Up (John 12:20-36)
Wedding Reception (John 2:1-11)	Who's Yer Daddy? (John 12:37-43)
Swap Meet (John 2:12-22)	Night Light (John 12:44-50)
Jesus Plays it Cool (John 2:23-25)	Party of 13 12 (John 13:1-35)
Nick at Night (John 3:1-21)	If I Had Just One More Night (John 13:36–14:31)
More/Not More (John 3:22-36)	Stick With It (John 15:1-8)
Woman@TheWell.com (John 4:1-42)	Seriously: Stick With Me (John 15:9-17)
I'll Take Your Word for That (John 4:43-54)	Father, Son, Holy Spirit + You (John 15:18-27)
Everyone Outta the Pool (John 5:1-15)	All for the Best (John 16:1-16)
Jesus Picks a Fight (John 5:16-47)	Lemme Give You His Direct Line (John 16:17-33)
5 Loaves, 2 Fishes, 12 Doggie Bags (John 6:1-15)	This One's for You (John 17:1-26)
Long Walk Off a Short Pier (John 6:16-21)	So It's Come to This (John 18:1-18)
Adventures in Missing the Point (John 6:22-34)	Trying Times (John 18:19-24)
You Want Bread? Here's Your Bread. (John 6:35-60)	Strike Three (John 18:25-27)
Where Else Would We Go? (John 6:61-71)	Trying Times II (John 18:28-40)
If I Needed This Kind of Abuse... (John 7:1-13)	The People's Court (John 19:1-6)
Word on the Street (John 7:14-36)	Crucified, Dead, and Buried (John 19:17-42)
Thirsty? (John 7:37-52)	Rise (John 20:1-9)
Caught with Their Pants Down (John 8:1-11)	Garden Party (John 20:10-18)
News at Six (John 8:12-59)	And Apparently He Also Walks Through Walls (John 20:19-31)
Sight for Sore Eyes (John 9:1-41)	Brunch at the Beach (John 21:1-14)
Making Metaphors (John 10:1-21)	Three Strikes and You're Still In (John 21:15-22)
I & the Father Are One: Deal With It (John 10:22-42)	Now What? (John 21:23-25)

● TIES AND TUGS—MYSPACE NOTES

● 25 GENTLE TUGS

(in no particular order)

- Is there anything that prevents you from trusting Jesus?

- When I finally got this story, I knew it was time to give my life to Jesus. Is this your time? Tell me what you mean.

- Tell me what you think about this story I've been telling you.

- How could you see this making a difference in your life?

- Am I making any sense at all?

- Can you see how this makes sense to me? Does it make sense to you? Tell me about that.

- What part of this makes the most sense to you?

- Are you getting your questions answered?

- Do you find God's Story hard to believe?

- Tell me where you're at with this God stuff.

- I'd love to know if God's Story is starting to connect with you.

- If you could ask God one question about all of this, what would you ask?

- What do you want to do about all of this?

- Have you told God what you're thinking?

- Tell me how God's Story is starting to be part of your story.

- I'm curious: Is it getting harder or easier for you to talk about God this way?

- Are there any questions you're waiting for Jesus to answer before you trust him?

- I remember being where you seem to be right now. Can I tell you that story?

- I remember the first time I talked to God—I mean really leveled with him. I said...

- I heard about a guy who got to a point where he was like 51 percent belief and 49 percent doubt, and he thought, "I believe it more than I doubt it and maybe that's enough to go on." (That guy, Don Finto, became pastor of the Belmont Church in Nashville, where doubters were always welcome.)

- I heard about a guy whose first real prayer was, "God, I feel like I've screwed up everything I've ever done. If you can do better, you're welcome to try." He said, "It wasn't incredibly deep, but apparently it was enough, because bit by bit, things started changing from then on." (That guy is a writer named Jim Hancock. He's spent most of his adult life helping people connect with God.)

- What's the hardest thing for you to believe about God's Story right now?

- Is there anything keeping you from putting your trust in Jesus?

- So on a scale of 1 to 5 (if 1 means "I don't believe it at all" and 5 means "I'm in"), where would you put yourself?

- Would you like to talk with Jesus about all of this? I'll join you, if you want.

●TAKIN' IT TO THE STREETS

Take a few minutes before you leave today to answer the following questions:

WHAT? What was the most significant thing you heard or did or thought about in L-Pod 6?

SO WHAT? Does anything you just wrote down require action?

NOW WHAT? What do you plan to do about that this week?

WHAT TEAM? Whom are you going to tell about your plans so they can help you through prayer and encouragement?

GOD'S STORY—ON YOUR OWN

A Sampler from John's Gospel
All for the Best (John 16:1-16)

"All this I have told you so that you will not fall away. They will put you out of the synagogue; in fact, the hour is coming when those who kill you will think they are offering a service to God. They will do such things because they have not known the Father or me. I have told you this, so that when their hour comes you will remember that I warned you about them. I did not tell you this from the beginning because I was with you, but now I am going to him who sent me. None of you asks me, 'Where are you going?' Rather, you are filled with grief because I have said these things. But very truly I tell you, it is for your good that I am going away. Unless I go away, the Advocate will not come to you; but if I go, I will send him to you. When he comes, he will prove the world to be in the wrong about sin and righteousness and judgment: about sin, because people do not believe in me; about righteousness, because I am going to the Father, where you can see me no longer; and about judgment, because the prince of this world now stands condemned.

"I have much more to say to you, more than you can now bear. But when he, the Spirit of truth, comes, he will guide you into all the truth. He will not speak on his own; he will speak only what he hears, and he will tell you what is yet to come. He will glorify me because it is from me that he will receive what he will make known to you. All that belongs to the Father is mine. That is why I said the Spirit will receive from me what he will make known to you."

Jesus went on to say, "In a little while you will see me no more, and then after a little while you will see me."

HMMM...
What truth—one that you need right now—can the Holy Spirit guide you toward?

GOD'S STORY—ON YOUR OWN

A Sampler from John's Gospel
This One's for You (John 17:1-26)

After Jesus said this, he looked toward heaven and prayed: "Father, the hour has come. Glorify your Son, that your Son may glorify you. For you granted him authority over all people that he might give eternal life to all those you have given him. Now this is eternal life: that they know you, the only true God, and Jesus Christ, whom you have sent. I have brought you glory on earth by finishing the work you gave me to do. And now, Father, glorify me in your presence with the glory I had with you before the world began.

"I have revealed you to those whom you gave me out of the world. They were yours; you gave them to me and they have obeyed your word. Now they know that everything you have given me comes from you. For I gave them the words you gave me and they accepted them. They knew with certainty that I came from you, and they believed that you sent me. I pray for them. I am not praying for the world, but for those you have given me, for they are yours. All I have is yours, and all you have is mine. And glory has come to me through them.

"I will remain in the world no longer, but they are still in the world, and I am coming to you. Holy Father, protect them by the power of your name, the name you gave me, so that they may be one as we are one. While I was with them, I protected them and kept them safe by that name you gave me. None has been lost except the one doomed to destruction so that Scripture would be fulfilled.

"I am coming to you now, but I say these things while I am still in the world, so that they may have the full measure of my joy within them. I have given them your word and the world has hated them, for they are not of the world any more than I am of the world. My prayer is not that you take them out of the world but that you protect them from the evil one. They are not of the world, even as I am not of it. Sanctify them by the truth; your word is truth. As you sent me into the world, I have sent them into the world. For them I sanctify myself, that they too may be truly sanctified.

"My prayer is not for them alone. I pray also for those who will believe in me through their message, that all of them may be one, Father, just as you are in me and I am in you. May they also be in us so that the world may believe that you have sent me. I have given them the glory that you gave me, that they may be one as we are one—I in them and you in me—so that they may be brought to complete unity. Then the world will know that you sent me and have loved them even as you have loved me.

"Father, I want those you have given me to be with me where I am, and to see my glory, the glory you have given me because you loved me before the creation of the world.

"Righteous Father, though the world does not know you, I know you, and they know that you have sent me. I have made you known to them, and will continue to make you known in order that the love you have for me may be in them and that I myself may be in them."

HMMM...
Jesus prays for you directly beginning in verse 20. How well do you make yourself available to work for and experience the unity for which he prays?

GOD'S STORY—ON YOUR OWN

A Sampler from John's Gospel
So It's Come to This (John 18:1-18)

When he had finished praying, Jesus left with his disciples and crossed the Kidron Valley. On the other side there was a garden, and he and his disciples went into it.

Now Judas, who betrayed him, knew the place, because Jesus had often met there with his disciples. So Judas came to the garden, guiding a detachment of soldiers and some officials from the chief priests and the Pharisees. They were carrying torches, lanterns and weapons.

Jesus, knowing all that was going to happen to him, went out and asked them, "Who is it you want?"

"Jesus of Nazareth," they replied.

"I am he," Jesus said. (And Judas the traitor was standing there with them.) When Jesus said, "I am he," they drew back and fell to the ground.

Again he asked them, "Who is it you want?"

"Jesus of Nazareth," they said.

Jesus answered, "I told you that I am he. If you are looking for me, then let these men go." This happened so that the words he had spoken would be fulfilled: "I have not lost one of those you gave me."

Then Simon Peter, who had a sword, drew it and struck the high priest's servant, cutting off his right ear. (The servant's name was Malchus.)

Jesus commanded Peter, "Put your sword away! Shall I not drink the cup the Father has given me?"

Then the detachment of soldiers with its commander and the Jewish officials arrested Jesus. They bound him and brought him first to Annas, who was the father-in-law of Caiaphas, the high priest that year. Caiaphas was the one who had advised the Jewish leaders that it would be good if one man died for the people.

Simon Peter and another disciple were following Jesus. Because this disciple was known to the high priest, he went with Jesus into the high priest's courtyard, but Peter had to wait outside at the door. The other disciple, who was known to the high priest, came back, spoke to the servant girl on duty there and brought Peter in.

"You aren't one of this man's disciples too, are you?" she asked Peter.

He replied, "I am not."

It was cold, and the servants and officials stood around a fire they had made to keep warm. Peter also was standing with them, warming himself.

HMMM...
What "sword" do you lean on—one that Jesus may want to take away so you can better learn his way?

By the grace of God, your friends may eventually choose to begin their own relationships with Jesus. So how can you help them to start well on this most incredible journey?

● BABY STEPS—MYSPACE NOTES

FROM THE LORD'S PRAYER

(The Other One)

John 17:14-19

I have given them your word and the world has hated them, for they are not of the world any more than I am of the world. My prayer is not that you take them out of the world but that you protect them from the evil one. They are not of the world, even as I am not of it. Sanctify them by the truth; your word is truth. As you sent me into the world, I have sent them into the world. For them I sanctify myself, that they too may be truly sanctified.

How we can join Jesus in this prayer:

Lord, thank you for giving us your Word. We know that the world has hated us, for we are not of the world any more than you are of the world. We agree that we don't want you to take us out of the world, but we confess we need you to protect us from the evil one. We know in our deepest souls that we are not of the world, even as you are not of it. Sanctify us by the truth; your Word is truth. And Father, as you sent Jesus into the world, we accept his assignment for us to be sent into the world, where our friends who don't know you still live in darkness. Thank you, Jesus, for setting yourself apart for us, so that we too may be truly set apart for you.

●HIGH POINTS OF GOD'S STORY

High Point #1

JESUS...

High Point #2

JESUS...

High Point #3

JESUS...

If you ever get lost while trying to recall parts of God's Story, just remember that it's all about Jesus.

GOD'S STORY

Jigsaw Bible Study—Piece #1

Read the following passage from 1 Corinthians 15:1-19 and answer the questions so you're ready to share insights with your Circle.

Now, brothers and sisters, I want to remind you of the gospel I preached to you, which you received and on which you have taken your stand. By this gospel you are saved, if you hold firmly to the word I preached to you. Otherwise, you have believed in vain.

For what I received I passed on to you as of first importance: that Christ died for our sins according to the Scriptures, that he was buried, that he was raised on the third day according to the Scriptures, and that he appeared to Cephas, and then to the Twelve. After that, he appeared to more than five hundred of the brothers and sisters at the same time, most of whom are still living, though some have fallen asleep. Then he appeared to James, then to all the apostles, and last of all he appeared to me also, as to one abnormally born.

For I am the least of the apostles and do not even deserve to be called an apostle, because I persecuted the church of God. But by the grace of God I am what I am, and his grace to me was not without effect. No, I worked harder than all of them—yet not I, but the grace of God that was with me. Whether, then, it is I or they, this is what we preach, and this is what you believed.

But if it is preached that Christ has been raised from the dead, how can some of you say that there is no resurrection of the dead? If there is no resurrection of the dead, then not even Christ has been raised. And if Christ has not been raised, our preaching is useless and so is your faith. More than that, we are then found to be false witnesses about God, for we have testified about God that he raised Christ from the dead. But he did not raise him if in fact the dead are not raised. For if the dead are not raised, then Christ has not been raised either. And if Christ has not been raised, your faith is futile; you are still in your sins. Then those also who have fallen asleep in Christ are lost. If only for this life we have hope in Christ, we are to be pitied more than all others.

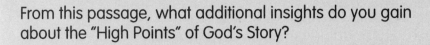

From this passage, what additional insights do you gain about the "High Points" of God's Story?

This is part of a letter written to a group of Christians. What are some of the problems that this section of the letter seems to address?

What—if anything—do you discover about the writer's story in this passage?

What does this passage say about the importance of Jesus' resurrection in regard to My Story?

GOD'S STORY

Jigsaw Bible Study—Piece #2

Read the following passage from Romans 6:1-10 and answer the questions so you're ready to share insights with your Circle.

What shall we say, then? Shall we go on sinning so that grace may increase? By no means! We are those who have died to sin; how can we live in it any longer? Or don't you know that all of us who were baptized into Christ Jesus were baptized into his death? We were therefore buried with him through baptism into death in order that, just as Christ was raised from the dead through the glory of the Father, we too may live a new life.

If we have been united with him in a death like his, we will certainly also be united with him in a resurrection like his. For we know that our old self was crucified with him so that the body ruled by sin might be done away with, that we should no longer be slaves to sin—because anyone who has died has been set free from sin.

Now if we died with Christ, we believe that we will also live with him. For we know that since Christ was raised from the dead, he cannot die again; death no longer has mastery over him. The death he died, he died to sin once for all; but the life he lives, he lives to God.

From this passage, what additional insights do you gain about the "High Points" of God's Story?

This is part of a letter written to a group of Christians. What are some of the problems that this section of the letter seems to address?

What—if anything—do you discover about the writer's story in this passage?

What does this passage say about the importance of Jesus' resurrection in regard to My Story?

GOD'S STORY

Jigsaw Bible Study—Piece #3

Read the following passage from Colossians 3:1-17 and answer the questions so you're ready to share insights with your Circle.

Since, then, you have been raised with Christ, set your hearts on things above, where Christ is seated at the right hand of God. Set your minds on things above, not on earthly things. For you died, and your life is now hidden with Christ in God. When Christ, who is your life, appears, then you also will appear with him in glory.

Put to death, therefore, whatever belongs to your earthly nature: sexual immorality, impurity, lust, evil desires and greed, which is idolatry. Because of these, the wrath of God is coming. You used to walk in these ways, in the life you once lived. But now you must also rid yourselves of all such things as these: anger, rage, malice, slander, and filthy language from your lips. Do not lie to each other, since you have taken off your old self with its practices and have put on the new self, which is being renewed in knowledge in the image of its Creator. Here there is no Gentile or Jew, circumcised or uncircumcised, barbarian, Scythian, slave or free, but Christ is all, and is in all.

Therefore, as God's chosen people, holy and dearly loved, clothe yourselves with compassion, kindness, humility, gentleness and patience. Bear with each other and forgive one another if any of you has a grievance against someone. Forgive as the Lord forgave you. And over all these virtues put on love, which binds them all together in perfect unity.

Let the peace of Christ rule in your hearts, since as members of one body you were called to peace. And be thankful. Let the message of Christ dwell among you richly as you teach and admonish one another with all wisdom through psalms, hymns and songs from the Spirit, singing to God with gratitude in your hearts. And whatever you do, whether in word or deed, do it all in the name of the Lord Jesus, giving thanks to God the Father through him.

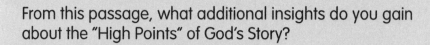

From this passage, what additional insights do you gain about the "High Points" of God's Story?

This is part of a letter written to a group of Christians. What are some of the problems that this section of the letter seems to address?

What—if anything—do you discover about the writer's story in this passage?

What does this passage say about the importance of Jesus' resurrection in regard to My Story?

GOD'S STORY

Jigsaw Bible Study—Piece #4

Read the following passage from Philippians 3:7-21 and answer the questions so you're ready to share insights with your Circle.

But whatever were gains to me I now consider loss for the sake of Christ. What is more, I consider everything a loss because of the surpassing worth of knowing Christ Jesus my Lord, for whose sake I have lost all things. I consider them garbage, that I may gain Christ and be found in him, not having a righteousness of my own that comes from the law, but that which is through faith in Christ—the righteousness that comes from God on the basis of faith. I want to know Christ—yes, to know the power of his resurrection and participation in his sufferings, becoming like him in his death, and so, somehow, attaining to the resurrection from the dead.

Not that I have already obtained all this, or have already arrived at my goal, but I press on to take hold of that for which Christ Jesus took hold of me. Brothers and sisters, I do not consider myself yet to have taken hold of it. But one thing I do: Forgetting what is behind and straining toward what is ahead, I press on toward the goal to win the prize for which God has called me heavenward in Christ Jesus.

All of us, then, who are mature should take such a view of things. And if on some point you think differently, that too God will make clear to you. Only let us live up to what we have already attained.

Join together in following my example, brothers and sisters, and just as you have us as a model, keep your eyes on those who live as we do. For, as I have often told you before and now tell you again even with tears, many live as enemies of the cross of Christ. Their destiny is destruction, their god is their stomach, and their glory is in their shame. Their mind is set on earthly things. But our citizenship is in heaven. And we eagerly await a Savior from there, the Lord Jesus Christ, who, by the power that enables him to bring everything under his control, will transform our lowly bodies so that they will be like his glorious body.

From this passage, what additional insights do you gain about the "High Points" of God's Story?

This is part of a letter written to a group of Christians. What are some of the problems that this section of the letter seems to address?

What—if anything—do you discover about the writer's story in this passage?

What does this passage say about the importance of Jesus' resurrection in regard to My Story?

GOD'S STORY

Jigsaw Bible Study—Putting It All Together

After about 12 minutes in individual study, pull everyone into the Circle to discuss what they've learned and how their findings help answer the following questions.

What are some additional insights about the "High Points" of God's Story?

What are some of the problems that these letters seem to address?

Which of these problems are still fairly common today?

The same person—the apostle Paul—wrote each of the four letters we studied. What have we discovered about Paul's story from these portions of his letters?

All of these passages were chosen because they address the topic of the resurrection of Jesus in some way. Taken together, what can we learn about the importance of Jesus' resurrection in regard to My Story?

● TAKIN' IT TO THE STREETS

Take a few minutes before you leave today to answer the following questions:

WHAT? What was the most significant thing you heard or did or thought about in L-Pod 7?

SO WHAT? Does anything you just wrote down require action?

NOW WHAT? What do you plan to do about that this week?

WHAT TEAM? Whom are you going to tell about your plans so they can help you through prayer and encouragement?

GOD'S STORY—ON YOUR OWN

A Sampler from John's Gospel
Crucified, Dead, and Buried (John 19:17-42)

Carrying his own cross, he went out to the place of the Skull (which in Aramaic is called Golgotha). Here they crucified him, and with him two others—one on each side and Jesus in the middle.

Pilate had a notice prepared and fastened to the cross. It read: JESUS OF NAZARETH, THE KING OF THE JEWS. Many of the Jews read this sign, for the place where Jesus was crucified was near the city, and the sign was written in Aramaic, Latin and Greek. The chief priests of the Jews protested to Pilate, "Do not write 'The King of the Jews,' but that this man claimed to be king of the Jews."

Pilate answered, "What I have written, I have written."

When the soldiers crucified Jesus, they took his clothes, dividing them into four shares, one for each of them, with the undergarment remaining. This garment was seamless, woven in one piece from top to bottom.

"Let's not tear it," they said to one another. "Let's decide by lot who will get it."

This happened that the scripture might be fulfilled that said, "They divided my clothes among them and cast lots for my garment."

So this is what the soldiers did.

Near the cross of Jesus stood his mother, his mother's sister, Mary the wife of Clopas, and Mary Magdalene. When Jesus saw his mother there, and the disciple whom he loved standing nearby, he said to her, "Woman, here is your son," and to the disciple, "Here is your mother." From that time on, this disciple took her into his home.

Later, knowing that everything had now been finished, and so that Scripture would be fulfilled, Jesus said, "I am thirsty." A jar of wine vinegar was there, so they soaked a sponge in it, put the sponge on a stalk of the hyssop plant, and lifted it to Jesus' lips. When he had received the drink, Jesus said, "It is finished." With that, he bowed his head and gave up his spirit.

Now it was the day of Preparation, and the next day was to be a special Sabbath. Because the Jewish leaders did not want the bodies left on the crosses during the Sabbath, they asked Pilate to have the legs broken and the bodies taken down. The soldiers therefore came and broke the legs of the first man who had been crucified with Jesus, and then those of the other. But when they came to Jesus and found that he was already dead, they did not break his legs. Instead, one of the soldiers pierced Jesus' side with a spear, bringing a sudden flow of blood and water. The man who saw it has given testimony, and his testimony is true. He knows that he tells the truth, and he testifies so that you also may believe. These things happened so that the scripture would be fulfilled: "Not one of his bones will be broken," and, as another scripture says, "They will look on the one they have pierced."

Later, Joseph of Arimathea asked Pilate for the body of Jesus. Now Joseph was a disciple of Jesus, but secretly because he feared the Jewish leaders. With Pilate's permission, he came and took the body away. He was accompanied by Nicodemus, the man who earlier had visited Jesus at night. Nicodemus brought a mixture of myrrh and aloes, about seventy-five pounds. Taking Jesus' body, the two of them wrapped it, with the spices, in strips of linen. This was in accordance with Jewish burial customs. At the place where Jesus was crucified, there was a garden, and in the garden a new tomb, in which no one had ever been laid. Because it was the Jewish day of Preparation and since the tomb was nearby, they laid Jesus there.

HMMM...
Look closely at all the people who are mentioned in the passage as standing around the cross while Jesus is being crucified. What do you imagine their lives were like after that experience?

GOD'S STORY—ON YOUR OWN

A Sampler from John's Gospel
And Apparently He Also Walks Through Walls (John 20:19-31)

On the evening of that first day of the week, when the disciples were together, with the doors locked for fear of the Jewish leaders, Jesus came and stood among them and said, "Peace be with you!" After he said this, he showed them his hands and side. The disciples were overjoyed when they saw the Lord.

Again Jesus said, "Peace be with you! As the Father has sent me, I am sending you." And with that he breathed on them and said, "Receive the Holy Spirit. If you forgive the sins of anyone, their sins are forgiven; if you do not forgive them, they are not forgiven."

Now Thomas (also known as Didymus), one of the Twelve, was not with the disciples when Jesus came. So the other disciples told him, "We have seen the Lord!"

But he said to them, "Unless I see the nail marks in his hands and put my finger where the nails were, and put my hand into his side, I will not believe."

A week later his disciples were in the house again, and Thomas was with them. Though the doors were locked, Jesus came and stood among them and said, "Peace be with you!" Then he said to Thomas, "Put your finger here; see my hands. Reach out your hand and put it into my side. Stop doubting and believe."

Thomas said to him, "My Lord and my God!"

Then Jesus told him, "Because you have seen me, you have believed; blessed are those who have not seen and yet have believed."

Jesus performed many other signs in the presence of his disciples, which are not recorded in this book. But these are written that you may believe that Jesus is the Messiah, the Son of God, and that by believing you may have life in his name.

HMMM...
Are you ready to be sent into the world of your friends, in the same way the Father sent Jesus to us? How ready are you?

GOD'S STORY—ON YOUR OWN

A Sampler from John's Gospel
Now What? (John 21:23-25)

Because of this, the rumor spread among the believers that this disciple would not die. But Jesus did not say that he would not die; he only said, "If I want him to remain alive until I return, what is that to you?"

This is the disciple who testifies to these things and who wrote them down. We know that his testimony is true.

Jesus did many other things as well. If every one of them were written down, I suppose that even the whole world would not have room for the books that would be written.

HMMM...
Why does Jesus want you to avoid comparing your experience as his follower with the experiences of other people?

:: L-POD 8 dimension

It might sometimes feel as though your friends' beginnings with Jesus signal the end of some exciting personal growth for you. So how can you get into a 3Story rhythm that leads you to a lifetime of adventure?

● DIMENSION

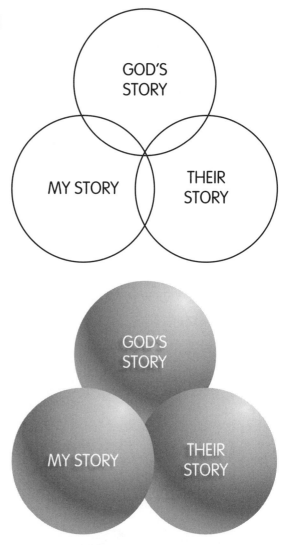

DIMENSION—MYSPACE NOTES

GOD'S STORY

Hearing from Jesus (John 21:1-25)

Afterward Jesus appeared again to his disciples, by the Sea of Galilee. It happened this way: Simon Peter, Thomas (also known as Didymus), Nathanael from Cana in Galilee, the sons of Zebedee, and two other disciples were together. "I'm going out to fish," Simon Peter told them, and they said, "We'll go with you." So they went out and got into the boat, but that night they caught nothing.

Early in the morning, Jesus stood on the shore, but the disciples did not realize that it was Jesus.

He called out to them, "Friends, haven't you any fish?"

"No," they answered.

He said, "Throw your net on the right side of the boat and you will find some." When they did, they were unable to haul the net in because of the large number of fish.

Then the disciple whom Jesus loved said to Peter, "It is the Lord!" As soon as Simon Peter heard him say, "It is the Lord," he wrapped his outer garment around him (for he had taken it off) and jumped into the water. The other disciples followed in the boat, towing the net full of fish, for they were not far from shore, about a hundred yards. When they landed, they saw a fire of burning coals there with fish on it, and some bread.

Jesus said to them, "Bring some of the fish you have just caught."

Simon Peter climbed aboard and dragged the net ashore. It was full of large fish, 153, but even with so many the net was not torn. Jesus said to them, "Come and have breakfast." None of the disciples dared ask him, "Who are you?" They knew it was the Lord. Jesus came, took the bread and gave it to them, and did the same with the fish. This was now the third time Jesus appeared to his disciples after he was raised from the dead.

When they had finished eating, Jesus said to Simon Peter, "Simon son of John, **do you love me** more than these?"

"Yes, Lord," he said, "You know that I love you."

Jesus said, "**Feed my lambs.**"

Again Jesus said, "Simon son of John, **do you love me?**"

He answered, "Yes, Lord, you know that I love you."

Jesus said, "**Take care of my sheep.**"

The third time he said to him, "Simon son of John, **do you love me?**"

Peter was hurt because Jesus asked him the third time, **"Do you love me?"** He said, "Lord, you know all things; you know that I love you."

Jesus said, "**Feed my sheep.** Very truly I tell you, when you were younger you dressed yourself and went where you wanted; but when you are old you will stretch out your hands, and someone else will dress you and lead you where you do not want to go." Jesus said this to indicate the kind of death by which Peter would glorify God. Then he said to him, "Follow me!"

Peter turned and saw that the disciple whom Jesus loved was following them. (This was the one who had leaned back against Jesus at the supper and had said, "Lord, who is going to betray you?") When Peter saw him, he asked, "Lord, what about him?"

Jesus answered, "If I want him to remain alive until I return, what is that to you? You must follow me." Because of this, the rumor spread among the believers that this disciple would not die. But Jesus did not say that he would not die; he only said, "If I want him to remain alive until I return, what is that to you?"

This is the disciple who testifies to these things and who wrote them down. We know that his testimony is true.

Jesus did many other things as well. If every one of them were written down, I suppose that even the whole world would not have room for the books that would be written.

PRACTICE: DIMENSION—GUIDED CONVERSATION #5

A Partnership Exercise (to be done on your own time)

- Tell each other the first name of the person you've been thinking about throughout the 3Story learning.

- Tell each other the story about how you met those people and got to know them.

- Tell each other how you realized your friends were still in need of rescue.

- Give each other a list of the issues you know your friends struggle with.

- Which of those issues have your friends talked with you about?

  - Where is that conversation as of right now?

- Have your friends closed the door on talking with you about any of those issues?

- Describe any fear you have about uncovering your story for your friends.

  - Where does that fear come from?

- Describe any fear you have about unfolding God's Story for your friends.

  - Where does that fear come from?

- Talk about connecting points you have with your friends— places where My Story and Their Story already match up.

- Talk about tie points between your friends and God—places where Their Story and God's Story already match up.

- Share some stories (that your friends don't already know) about your present-tense need for Jesus.

  - Is there anything that would keep you from uncovering those stories for your friends?

- If you could ask God for one thing for your friends right now, what would that be?

TAKIN' IT TO THE STREETS

Take a few minutes before you leave today to answer the following questions:

WHAT? What was the most significant thing you heard or did or thought about in L-Pod 8?

SO WHAT? Does anything you just wrote down require action?

NOW WHAT? What do you plan to do about that this week?

WHAT TEAM? Whom are you going to tell about your plans so they can help you through prayer and encouragement?

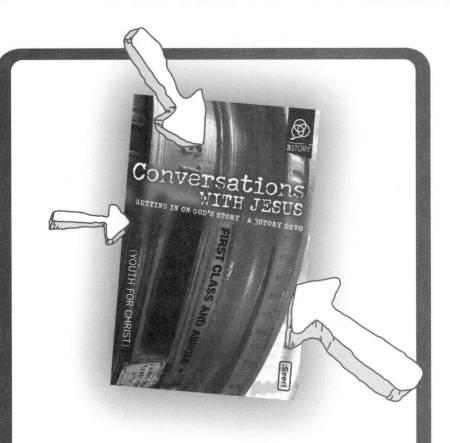

LISTEN TO WHAT JESUS HAS TO SAY TO YOU. IN THIS 60-DAY DEVO YOU'LL RECEIVE DAILY LETTERS FROM JESUS AND SPEND SOME TIME JOURNALING YOUR THOUGHTS BACK TO HIM AS YOU TAKE PART IN THE CONVERSATION.

Conversations with Jesus
Getting in on God's Story
Youth for Christ

RETAIL $10.99
ISBN 0-310-27346-3

invert